Weight Training

consultant:

Patrick Mediate
State Director Committee Chair
National Strength and Conditioning Association
Fairfield, Connecticut

LifeMatters
an imprint of Capstone Press
Mankato, Minnesota

by
Gus
Gedatus

LifeMatters Books are published by Capstone Press
PO Box 669 • 151 Good Counsel Drive • Mankato, Minnesota 56002
http://www.capstone-press.com

SPECIAL ADVISORY AND DISCLAIMER: The information within this book addresses fitness and sports activities that carry significant safety risks, including the risk of serious personal injury. Because this book is general in nature, we recommend that the reader seek qualified professional instruction and advice. We also recommend the use of quality protective equipment when participating in fitness and sports activities. The publisher, its consultants, and the author take no responsibility for the use of any of the materials or methods described in this book nor for the products thereof.

Printed in the United States of America

Library of Congress Cataloging-in-Publication Data
Gedatus, Gustav Mark.
     Weight training / by Gus Gedatus.
              p.   cm. — (Nutrition and fitness)
     Includes bibliographical references and index.
     ISBN 0-7368-0708-X
     1. Weight training for children—Juvenile literature. 2. Physical fitness for children—Juvenile literature.
     [1. Weight training. 2. Physical fitness. 3. Nutrition.] I. Title. II. Series.
     GV546.6.C45 G43 2001
     613.7´13—dc21
                                    00-010923
                                    CIP

     Summary: Explains how weight training contributes to fitness; talks about toning vs. building muscle, proper nutrition, supplements, and setting up a program; describes how to lift and gives examples of basic exercises.

Staff Credits
Rebecca Aldridge, editor; Adam Lazar, designer and illustrator; Kim Danger, photo researcher

Photo Credits
Cover: Stock Market Photo/©Mug Shots
©Artville/Clair Alaska, 28
Index Stock Photos/©SW Production, 7; ©BSIP Agency, 27; ©Lucille Khornak, 37, 46; ©Donald Graham, 43; ©Jack Gescheidt, 45
Pictor/©Daemmrich, 8
Unicorn Stock Photos/©Martin R. Jones, 12; ©Karen Holsinger Mullen, 30; ©Dick Young, 34; ©Paul Murphy, 51; ©Chris Boylan, 53
Uniphoto/©Andy Anderson, 39; ©Ed Elberfeld, 59
Visuals Unlimited/©D. Yeske, 15; ©Kenneth Greer, 21; ©Dick Thomas, 55

A 0 9 8 7 6 5 4 3 2 1

Table of Contents

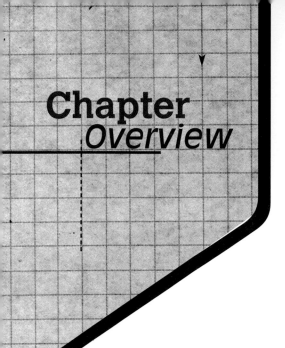

Chapter Overview

- When you're fit, all systems of your body operate at their best.

- Overall fitness training includes both aerobic and anaerobic exercise.

- Weight training provides many benefits such as toned muscles, weight control, and possibly even lower risk of certain diseases.

- Weight lifting, power lifting, and bodybuilding are not the same as weight training. Lifting and building focus on lifting very heavy weights and building muscles. Weight training focuses on using lighter weights to strengthen muscles, improve performance, and prevent injury.

Chapter 1

What Weight Training Can Do for You

Exercise and Fitness

Being fit means that your body organs and systems are in good shape and work efficiently. Usually, it means you have a lot of energy because your body is working well. Many health professionals believe that a truly fit person has the right amount of muscle compared to body fat. By staying fit, you're likely to remain healthy and avoid injury throughout your life.

A total fitness program includes exercises that are aerobic and others that are anaerobic. Each of these types of exercise benefits the body in a different way.

Aerobic exercise is great for strengthening the heart and lungs and lowering body fat. It speeds up your breathing process, working your heart and lungs harder than usual. Over time, your heart is able to pump more blood more easily. Your lungs are able to take in a greater amount of air. At the same time, your muscles use oxygen and burn calories. These are the units of energy that come from the food you eat. Therefore, aerobic exercise helps you lose fat and tone muscle. Bicycling, in-line skating, and aerobic dancing are some examples of aerobic exercise.

Any regular exercise can help you with your ability to focus and to concentrate. That means a weight training program might even help you do better in school.

Anaerobic exercise, such as weight training, works the body in a different way. Unlike aerobic exercise, anaerobic exercise doesn't use a lot of oxygen. For example, when doing a set of repeated lifts, you must stop to take a breath. As you press your muscles to work against the extra weight, you work beyond your ability to breathe normally. Then, you burn carbohydrates. The more the muscles work, the better developed they become. Muscle mass increases and muscles become more toned. Then muscles are better able to work for you as fat burners. That's because muscle burns more calories at rest than fat does.

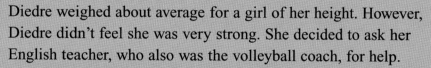

Diedre, Age 16

Diedre weighed about average for a girl of her height. However, Diedre didn't feel she was very strong. She decided to ask her English teacher, who also was the volleyball coach, for help.

With Ms. Lawson's advice, Diedre started an exercise program that included weight training. Ms. Lawson showed Diedre how to do some weight training exercises. Ms. Lawson also told Diedre that setting some goals might be helpful. Diedre made one of her goals getting the afterschool job she wanted. It involved lifting boxes.

After a few weeks, Diedre noticed that her muscles seemed firmer. Once she had developed some confidence in her ability to lift boxes, Diedre interviewed for the job. Now she is eagerly continuing her weight training. And she loves her new job.

Weight training can improve your performance in other sports.

Why Weight Training?

You're already aware of some anaerobic benefits of weight training. But weight training can do a lot of other good things for you and your body. If you are or want to be an athletic person, weight training can help you perform better in other sports. You probably will be able to run faster, jump higher, hit a ball harder, or throw it farther. That's because a regular program of weight training can increase your endurance and strength for other sports. Weight training can help you with simple, everyday tasks, too. Your body probably won't be as stressed when you carry a backpack or heavy bags of groceries.

People who weight train reduce their chance for injury in other sports. With stronger muscles from weight training, you're less likely to suffer a sprain. You may take part in a new activity that you aren't used to. Stronger muscles can help you avoid aches and pains the next day.

Some studies show that weight training may reduce levels of unhealthy cholesterol in the blood. The body needs some cholesterol. However, too much of this waxy substance can lead to heart disease.

Weight training can maintain or increase bone density. This means that bones remain strong. With dense, healthy bones, you're less likely to suffer a bone fracture, or crack. This is important because without exercise, our bones lose density as we age. Weight training also reduces the risk of osteoporosis, a condition in which bones become fragile.

Weight lifting is a competitive sport. It is not the same as weight training.

For people who are concerned with improving the way they look, weight training can certainly help with that, too. Weight training, like all physical activity, burns calories so it helps control body weight. It tones and defines muscles, so they look strong and firm.

Toning vs. Building Muscle

Strengthening muscles without making them bigger is toning. Toned muscles are firm. In some people, they may even appear slightly smaller than muscles that aren't toned. That's because in-shape muscles occupy less space. For toning, you start with very light weights. Then you work on increasing the number of times you lift these light weights. After that you can move on to slightly heavier weights. For the best results, always use weights that are manageable and don't cause too much strain.

Making muscles larger is sometimes called building bulk. To do this, a person starts with light weights and advances to much heavier weights later. The person pushes himself or herself beyond what is truly a manageable weight for him or her. As the muscles get stronger, the person continues to increase the amount of weight used.

Some females may be afraid of weight training. They may think that it will give them big, bulging veins and muscles. This isn't likely to happen. For both men and women, the bodybuilder look requires strict dieting and almost daily lifting with maximum weights.

Teen Talk

Weight Training Is Not Competitive Lifting or Bodybuilding

Weight training is a part of improving overall fitness. It's also known as strength training. Weight training is different from weight lifting, power lifting, and bodybuilding. These all are competitive sports. They aren't recommended for teens because teens are still growing. An injury from lifting a heavy weight can permanently damage bones, joints, and tendons that aren't fully developed. You may really like weight training and decide that lifting or bodybuilding is something you want to get into. If so, a doctor can tell you when your body is fully developed and ready to train for such competitive sports.

You can, however, do Olympic weight-lifting movements for form and technique using very light weights. This can help develop your motor pattern for later on. For example, take some children in Eastern Europe and the Middle East. As early as age 8, they begin training with broomsticks and bars to master movements used in weight lifting. They don't lift weights that are more than 30 percent of their own body weight until it's safe. Usually, this is around age 17, when their growth plates have formed fully.

Points to Consider

- What does being physically fit mean to you?

- If you were to start a weight training program, what would you hope to accomplish?

- Do you have an impression of people who lift weights? What is that impression?

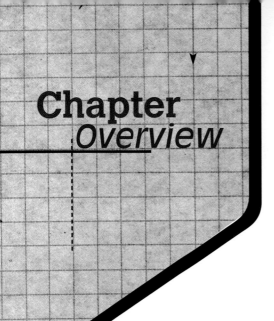

Chapter
Overview

- A good diet is important to achieve overall fitness and health.

- Proteins, carbohydrates, and vitamins are important nutrients for exercise. Food guides can help you decide which foods and how much of each to eat daily.

- Your eating habits can contribute to your fitness and health.

- Protein powders, drinks, and bars aren't necessary for teens who eat a balanced diet.

- Getting enough vitamins can help you succeed with a weight training program.

Chapter 2

The Importance of Diet

A weight training program can help you to develop your muscles. As your muscles become more efficient, they will burn more calories. However, that doesn't mean you can eat whatever foods you may want in any quantity. Whether or not you're in a weight training program, a lifetime pattern of healthy eating is important. A healthy, balanced diet and the right exercise plan work together to improve your total fitness. One without the other rarely does the job.

The Best Food Choices

The food choices for complementing a weight training program are pretty simple. Complex carbohydrates such as breads, cereals, rice, pastas, and potatoes supply long-lasting energy for the body. They produce sugar, or glucose, for every cell. Complex carbohydrates are the most efficiently burned fuel for the body. Much of the energy for your workouts comes from complex carbohydrates.

Fruits and vegetables provide the body with needed vitamins, minerals, and fiber.

Proteins repair injured muscle fiber and help build new muscle. They build red blood cells and important body tissues. Proteins are found in lean meat such as the white meat of poultry, white fishes, egg whites, and skim milk. The highest amounts of protein can be found in meat and dairy foods, but these foods often have a high amount of fat. It's a good idea to get some of your protein from beans, rice, wheat, and nuts.

Fruits and vegetables supply your body with important vitamins and minerals. Vitamins are needed for specific body functions. Minerals are elements found in the earth that the body needs for good health. Fruits and vegetables also provide fiber that helps your digestive system to work its best. Fruits and vegetables require more energy to digest than other foods do. That means they increase the rate at which calories are burned.

If you want to control the amount of fat your body produces, limit the amount of fat you eat. This includes fried foods, oils, red meats, and processed meat and cheese products. It also includes dairy foods that aren't low-fat or nonfat. All forms of sugar are potential fat builders, too. An extra candy bar or pack of doughnuts doesn't contribute to fitness.

Ramundo, Age 15

Ramundo does his weight training in the morning. Usually, he has a doughnut and a glass of soda pop for breakfast about an hour before his workout. Ramundo thought that working out in the morning would give him more energy for the school day. However, by 10 A.M., he usually feels run down.

Ramundo decides to talk with the school nurse. She tells him that eating breakfast and working out are good for him. However, he isn't eating any snacks, so he isn't refueling his body until lunchtime. Also, what Ramundo eats for breakfast is a problem. Sure the sugar provides energy, but it's quick energy that doesn't last. Ramundo needs a complex carbohydrate at breakfast and then a healthy snack at about 10 A.M. to keep him going.

Now, Ramundo has two pieces of whole-grain toast with peanut butter and a glass of nonfat milk for breakfast. For a midmorning snack, he has a banana or some granola. He doesn't feel so sleepy during history class anymore!

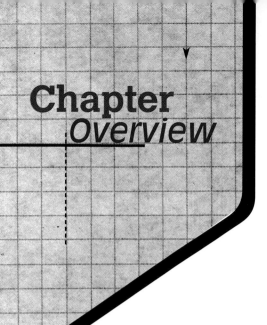

Chapter
Overview

- Some people take supplements to make weight training programs more effective.

- The three main types of supplements are anabolic, ergogenic, and thermogenic.

- Steroids are drugs that may help to increase muscle development. However, they produce many unwanted and dangerous side effects.

- DHEA and creatine are two popular supplements. They are not drugs. However, not enough tests have been done to show whether they are safe for teens to use.

Chapter 3

Supplements

Some people choose to take supplements to help make their weight training programs more effective. Most health experts do not recommend that teens use these supplements. Instead, experts suggest concentrating on eating right, drinking plenty of water, and possibly taking a multivitamin. These really are the only things you need to make working out effective.

So, what are supplements? Basically, there are three types. Anabolic supplements help with muscle building. Ergogenic supplements enhance workout performance. Thermogenic supplements put the metabolism to work at a higher rate. Metabolism is the process of the body changing calories to energy.

Becoming familiar with some basic terms may help as you set up your own weight training program. It will make it easier for you to learn about weight training. You'll be able to talk and write clearly about what you're doing. Following are some words that are commonly used. As you continue with your reading, it may help to refer back to this list.

Common Weight Training Terms

Circuit	A group of exercises you do in a certain order to strengthen different sets of muscles
Contracting a muscle	Shortening the muscle fibers by squeezing them together; the opposite of this is stretching, which extends muscle fibers.
Exercise	A movement for a specific muscle, intended to develop and strengthen that muscle
Intensity	The degree of difficulty of an exercise program; this can be determined by the type of exercise, number of reps and sets, amount of weight, and rests taken.
Repetition or rep	One complete exercise from start to middle to finish
Resistance	The heaviness, or amount of weight, of an object used for a certain exercise
Rest	A pause between sets of exercises; it gives the muscle a chance to recover, so it can efficiently do the next set.
Routine	A combination of exercises meant to benefit a certain body part
Set	A planned number of repetitions done without a rest
Split routine	A plan that includes working only certain body areas on certain days
Spotting	Standing near someone who is lifting to help the person safely follow through with a lift
Workout	All exercise performed on a certain day

Weight Training

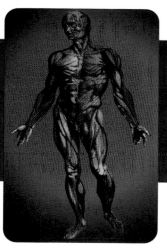

Weight training exercises work different muscles of the body.

Your Muscles and What They're Called

How familiar are you with the muscles in your body? Take a look at the chart below. It can give you an idea of which muscles you'll be working.

Body Muscles

Muscle	Location
Abdominals (abs)	Stomach
Gluteus maximus (glutes)	Buttocks (the fleshy part of the body on which you sit)
Hamstrings (hams)	Back of the thigh
Quadriceps (quads)	Front of the thigh
Lattisimus dorsi (lats)	Back
Pectorals (pecs)	Chest
Trapezius (traps)	Area from the shoulder to neck
Deltoids (delts)	Shoulders
Calves	Back of lower leg
Biceps	Front of the upper arm
Triceps	Back of the upper arm

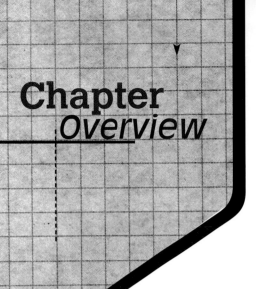

Chapter
Overview

- Warming up and stretching prepare your muscles for your weight training workout and help to prevent injury.

- A spotter is important for safety and encouragement.

- A proper lift includes exhaling as you lift and inhaling as you return to your starting position. It also includes using slow, even movements, good posture, and correct form. It's important to use a full range of motion, too.

- Resting between sets gives your muscles a chance to regain energy for the next set. The more weight you train with, the longer the rest period should be.

Chapter 5

Rules to Lift By

No matter which muscle you're working, certain rules can help you get the most from your workout. Many of these rules can help you avoid injury, too. These ideas may seem odd at first. However, once you get into your program, they probably will seem natural. As you begin your workout, keep the following activities in mind.

Warm Up and Stretch

Warm up and stretch before you start your weight training workout. It's a good idea to warm up for about 5 to 10 minutes. A warm-up might include easy aerobic exercise such as jogging or biking. Then it's important to stretch. This gets your muscles ready for the workout ahead and can help prevent injury. It's important to do some gentle stretches after a workout, too. This helps your muscles cool down gradually. A few examples of stretches follow. Ask a physical education teacher, a sports coach, or a certified trainer for examples of other stretches for different muscles.

Stretching before training with weights prepares muscles and helps prevent injury.

Stretch It Out!

Side Stretch

- Stand with your arms at your sides.

- Reach your left arm down the outside of your left leg. Your other arm should remain relaxed at your side. Hold the left arm stretch for 10 to 20 seconds.

- Repeat with the right arm and leg.

Triceps Stretch

- Raise your left arm over your head. Bend your arm at the elbow so your hand is behind your head.

- With your right hand, gently pull your left elbow to the right until you can feel the stretch.

- Hold for 10 to 20 seconds. Then repeat with the opposite arm.

Thigh Stretch

- Stand with legs slightly bent and your back straight.

- Bend your left knee. Hold the ankle of the left leg and gently pull your foot toward your buttocks. Keep your knee pointing straight down toward the floor. Once you feel the stretch, hold it for 10 to 20 seconds.

- Repeat with the right leg.

Weight Training

"When I first started doing curls to work my biceps, I thought my arms were going to fall off. Then I read somewhere that many people grip the bar the wrong way. I learned to relax my grip and make a hollow space with my hand. Then the barbell can move freely. Once I got rid of that stress in my hands, it was a breeze. My arms didn't hurt at all."—Cory, age 16

Work With a Spotter

Spotters are important, especially when you're working with free weights. Spotters help you safely handle weight during a workout. For example, you may get tired during a lift. If this happens, a spotter can keep you from dropping a barbell on yourself. Having a spotter also provides encouragement and a way to spend time with friends who weight train.

Inhale and Exhale

Don't hold your breath when you lift. Many people do this automatically. However, it can cause muscles to tense up and can harm form. Try to inhale, or breathe in, during the easier part of the exercise movement. Exhale, or breathe out, as you put the most effort into your move.

Staying relaxed while you work with weights can help you breathe normally. You may be less likely to tense up your face and grit your teeth. Being relaxed can help you not to put too much pressure on the bar as you hold it.

Use Slow, Even Movements

Don't rush your reps. Try to set a nice, slow, consistent rhythm. Perhaps count from one to five during each rep. If this is hard to do, you may be lifting too much weight too fast. Choose a lighter weight. After the first several reps, you should feel the muscle as you work it. If not, you're probably doing your reps too fast. When you do reps too fast, you don't get as much benefit from them.

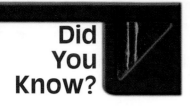

Syed, Age 16

Syed began weight training a year ago. He goes to the community center a few times a week. When Syed first started weight training, he just began by doing moves he saw other people do. After a couple of months, it didn't seem like he was seeing much improvement, and he was sore a lot.

One day, Jason, one of the staff at the center, came up to Syed while he was doing his workout. "You know, if you did that more slowly, you'd get better results," he told Syed. "Really?" Syed asked. "I thought it was just important to do a whole bunch."

"Nah, it's better to do less weight more slowly. That way your muscle develops properly," Jason said.

Jason helped Syed with some good exercises and demonstrated proper form. In a few weeks, Syed could see changes in himself. And his workouts didn't leave his muscles aching anymore. He wished he had talked with somebody like Jason sooner.

Good posture and smooth and controlled movements help you to get the most benefit from a weight training session.

Use Good Form

Good posture is essential for getting the most out of your workout. Machines put your body in the proper alignment. Free weights require effort to maintain form. If you don't use good posture, you could injure yourself. In standing exercises, you should stand with your back perfectly straight, your shoulders back, and your chest out. Your legs should be straight but not locked.

Keep control of your form. Your movements should be smooth and controlled, not jerky. If the weight you're using is too much, it may affect your form. Don't sacrifice form to get through a set. It's better to stop even before finishing a set than to continue doing an exercise incorrectly.

Use a Full Range of Motion

It's important to get the fullest range of motion possible for each exercise. If the fullest range isn't possible, then use a lighter weight. Again, don't sacrifice form for handling more weight than you can manage comfortably. At the top or bottom of a movement, don't hold the weight. Instead, keep moving constantly so that you keep the pressure on your muscles through an entire set. Delayed muscle soreness can occur if your negative, or lowering, movement is too slow.

Don't ever rest the bar of a weight on your chest or lock your elbows and hold the bar out or up. These movements can cause injury. Avoid making abrupt movements with weights. These moves can cause injury to ligaments or muscles. Ligaments are the tough bands of tissue that connect bones and hold some body organs in place.

It's important to rest between sets. This gives your muscles time to recover for the next set.

Give It a Rest

Muscles need time to rest. Between each set, take a break of 1 to 1½ minutes. After a hard workout, your muscles need 48 hours to recover. That means that weight training three times a week is about right. If you weight train more than that, you run the risk of injury. You can actually wear down muscles if you don't give them sufficient time to rest and grow.

Points to Consider

- Why do you think correct form is important?

- Do you think weight training could improve your posture? Why or why not?

- In your opinion, what are the three most important "rules to lift by"?

Carrying a heavy backpack can help you develop your trapezoids.

Free-Weight Exercises

There are many effective free-weight exercises to try. The following exercises are good ones that can help get you started. As you become comfortable with these exercises, you can learn countless others. These other exercises can help develop different muscles in your body and add great variety to your workout sessions.

For the Back and Shoulders

Overhead Presses (Benefit the deltoids.)

- Hold a barbell behind your head. Keep your hands wide apart and use an overhand grip (palms facing forward). Inhale.

- Exhale as you press the barbell overhead until your arms are almost locked.

- Lower the barbell to the starting position. Don't let the barbell rest on your neck. This could cause injury.

Rows (Benefit the trapezoids and deltoids.)

- Stand with feet shoulder-width apart.

- Hold a barbell (or dumbbells) in front of you and at your thighs. Use an overhand grip (palms facing toward your body), and keep your hands about 10 inches or 25 centimeters apart. Inhale.

- Exhale as you pull the barbell or dumbbells up gently to your chin.

- Bring the barbell or dumbbells to your starting position.

During free-weight exercises such as the bench press, a spotter can help. He or she can encourage you and keep you from dropping a weight on yourself if you tire.

For the Chest and Arms

Bench Presses (Benefit the pectorals and triceps.)

- Lie flat on your back on a bench. Keep knees bent and feet flat on the floor. When doing a bench press, make sure to keep your back against the bench. Arching your back can injure the lower back.

- Hold a barbell or two dumbbells at arm's length above the upper chest area. (If using a barbell, you will take the barbell from the rack above you and the bench you're lying on.) With a barbell, hands should be more than shoulder-width apart. Your grip should have palms facing up with thumbs around the bar. With dumbbells, hands should be shoulder-width apart.

- Inhale and lower the barbell or dumbbells to the midchest.

- As soon as the bar or weight touches your chest, press it upward again and exhale. The movement, as seen from the side, should be a smooth curve from the arm's-length position to the chest-touch position.

In an inclined bench press, you slightly raise the portion of the bench under your upper body. You most likely will lift less weight, but this exercise will benefit the upper pectorals.

When doing sit-ups, don't sit all the way up to the knees.

For the Abdominals

A strong stomach can provide an important foundation for your upper-body strength. In addition to helping flatten your stomach, building your stomach muscles reduces strain on your lower back. This is especially true for upper-body movements that are centered near the waist. For this reason, strong stomach muscles can aid you in many physical activities.

For strengthening and toning your upper abs, sit-ups or variations on them are the easiest and most effective exercise. When doing a sit-up, lie flat on the floor. Support your head by placing your hands behind your ears. Don't lock your hands behind your head. This strains your back. Raise your upper body off the floor at least enough to get your shoulders off the floor. However, don't sit up all the way to the knees. Use only your stomach muscles to raise yourself. Try to keep your legs on the floor. Lower yourself to the floor and repeat.

For strengthening your lower abs, lie on your back. Your arms should be at your sides with your palms touching the floor or mat. Raise your legs upward about 2 feet or .5 meters. Keep your upper body on the floor and your legs straight. You can do one leg at a time, and then slightly cross it to the side. This works the sides of your lower abs.

Crunches are half sit-ups that work your entire abdominals. With crunches, you don't move all the way up or down. These put continuous stress on your abs. As you lift and lower yourself slightly, looking and focusing on one spot on the ceiling may help.

Pull-ups, chin-ups, dips, and push-ups use body weight as resistance and are really good exercises for teens.

Did You Know?

Clarice, Age 17

Since she was little, Clarice had taken ballet lessons. She was small but she had strong foot arches. She was successful at ballet and was a good ice and in-line skater, too.

When Clarice decided to begin weight training, she had a specific plan. She wanted to strengthen her arms and back. Although she focused on her upper body, she worked on all of her muscle groups.

Clarice started her weight training with the very lightest weights, both in the dumbbells and barbells she used. In two years, she has increased the weight she lifts only slightly. However, her excellent form and her consistency in working out have made her muscles strong and firm.

Points to Consider

- Are there certain muscles on which you would like to concentrate? What is your reason for this?

- Do you think weight training takes the same amount of concentration as other forms of exercise? Why or why not?

- In what ways do you think a spotter could be helpful while doing the exercises explained in this chapter?

"I've been working out with free weights since I was 17 years old. I still do. People may think I'm a foolish old man. But I have never broken a bone, and I still play tennis three times a week."
—Charles, age 77

Take Advantage of Your Surroundings

If you love the outdoors, arrange to do your weight training outdoors. It may give you a special energy during your workouts. If you love water, try to work with free weights near water, even if only occasionally.

As you get older, you may travel a lot. This can get tricky, in terms of using weights. However, as mentioned earlier, there are many practical, inexpensive resistance systems that use bands and cords. You can take these with you practically anywhere. Then you can continue with your fitness training even while you're away from home.

If you do visit new places, take advantage of what the area has to offer. Maybe you'll find yourself near water. If so, you might want to try canoeing, surfing, windsurfing, or water skiing. Likewise, you may spend time in a snowy area. You might want to try skiing or snowshoeing. By trying new things, you may discover a new passion for an enjoyable fitness activity for life.

The bottom line is having a basic fitness level that can make new and exciting activities great fun. Fitness activities can add new dimension to your life. They can give you more reasons to laugh and spend time with friends. They can help you to stay healthy as you grow older.

Keep weight training fun and interesting—vary where you work out and try new exercises.

Points to Consider

- As you consider setting up your own weight training program, which part presents the greatest challenge to you?

- List a few early workout goals that you might set for yourself.

- What are some things that you could write about in your workout journal?

- If you became discouraged with your weight training program, what could you do to help change your attitude?

- What words of encouragement would you give someone else about starting a weight training program?

anaerobic (AN-air-oh-bik)—not requiring oxygen, or air

carbohydrate (kar-boh-HYE-drate)—a substance in foods such as bread, rice, pasta, and potatoes that provides energy

endurance (en-DUR-uhnss)—the ability to continue through a physically stressful activity

hormone (HOR-mohn)—a chemical made in the body that controls body development and functions

hydrate (HYE-drate)—to add water to something

intensity (in-TEN-suh-tee)—the degree of strength, force, energy, or feeling

metabolism (muh-TAB-uh-liz-uhm)—the process by which the body changes the food we eat into energy

protein (PROH-teen)—a substance that aids in building and repairing body tissue; protein is found in meat, dairy foods, beans, and nuts.

rep (REP)—one complete motion of an exercise from start to middle to finish; rep is short for repetition.

resistance (ri-ZISS-tuhnss)—a force that opposes the motion of an object

set (SET)—a planned number of exercise repetitions performed without a rest

spotting (SPOT-ing)—watching someone lift a weight to provide encouragement and help if the person tires

supplement (SUHP-luh-muhnt)—something added to complete another thing or to make up for something that is missing

tendinitis (ten-duh-NYE-tuhss)—swelling and pain in a band that joins a muscle to a bone or other body part

testosterone (tess-TAHSS-tuh-rohn)—a male sex hormone

Index

abdominals (abs), 27, 29, 46, 49, 52–54
aerobic exercise, 5, 33, 50, 55
anabolic supplements, 19–21, 23
anaerobic exercise, 5–8. *See also* weight training
arms, 27, 35, 42, 43–44, 49, 51
attitude, 55–56

back, 27, 29, 42, 43, 46, 51
bands, 29, 58
barbells, 29, 31, 35, 42–45, 47
bench presses, 43, 52–54
biceps, 27, 35, 44
bodybuilding, 8, 9, 22
bones, 7, 9, 38, 58
breathing, 5, 6, 35
building bulk, 8
buttocks, 27

calf raises, 45, 52–54
calories, 5, 6, 8, 11, 12, 16, 19
calves, 27, 45
carbohydrates, 6, 14, 15, 16–17
    complex, 11, 13
chest, 27, 43–44, 51
cholesterol, 7
circuit, 26
commitment, 49, 57
consistency, 47
contracting, 26
cords, 29, 58
creatine monohydrate, 22
crunches, 46, 52–54
curls, 35, 44, 52–54

deltoids (delts), 27, 42
DHEA, 21, 22
diet, 5, 11–17, 19, 49, 55
digestion, 12, 15, 16–17
dumbbells, 29, 42–44, 47

encouragement, 35, 56
energy, 5, 11, 12, 13, 15, 16–17, 19, 55, 58
energy drinks and bars, 16
equipment, 28, 29–30. *See also* bands; cords; free weights; machines, exercise
ergogenic supplements, 19

fat, 5, 6, 12, 14, 15, 56
food groups, 14. *See also* diet
food guides, 14
form, 28, 29, 35, 36, 37, 38, 42–46, 47
free weights, 29–30, 31, 37, 52
    exercises with, 41–47
fruits and vegetables, 12, 13, 14, 15, 16, 17

gluteus maximus (glutes), 27
goals, 6, 49, 51, 55
gym, 30–31

hamstrings (hams), 27, 45
health, 5, 7, 20, 21, 22, 50

injury prevention, 5, 7, 28, 33, 34, 36, 38, 39, 43
intensity, 26
isolation, 41

journals, 55, 57

Index

legs, 27, 45, 49, 51

machines, exercise, 30–31, 37, 52–54
minerals, 12, 17
multivitamins, 17, 19
muscle, 5, 38, 39, 56
    names of, 27
    strengthening, 7, 8, 25, 46, 47, 49
    toning, 5, 6, 8, 46, 51
myths, 56

overhead presses, 42, 52–54

patience, 55
pectoral (pecs), 27, 43
posture, 28, 37
power lifting, 9
protein powder, 16
proteins, 12, 14, 15, 16

quadriceps (quads), 27, 34, 45

range of motion, full, 38
relaxing, 35
repetition or rep, 26, 35, 41, 50, 52–54, 57
resistance, 26, 45, 47. *See also* bands; cords
rest, 26, 39, 50, 53
reverse curls, 44, 52–54
routine, 26, 28, 52–54
rows, 42

safety, 28
set, 26, 37, 38–39, 41, 50, 52–54
shoulders, 27, 42, 44, 45
sit-ups, 46

soreness, 7, 35, 36, 38, 56
split routine, 26, 51
sports, 7, 8, 9, 28, 49, 58
spotting, 26, 28, 35, 43, 45
squats, 45, 52–54
steroids, 20–21, 22
strength training. *See* weight training
stretching, 26, 28, 33, 34
supplements, 19–23

tendinitis, 36
testosterone, 20
thermogenic supplements, 19
trapezius (traps), 27, 42
travel, 58
triceps, 27, 34, 43, 44, 45, 52–54
triceps extensions, 44

vitamins, 12, 16–17

warm-ups, 28, 33, 50
water, 16, 19, 22
weight, body, 6, 8, 47, 56
weight lifting, 9
weight training, 55
    basics, 25–31
    program, 6, 11, 13, 16, 26, 28, 42–47, 49–59
    rules, 33–39
    what it can do for you, 5–9
workout, 19, 26. *See also* weight training, program
    change in, 49, 55, 57
    length of, 50
    schedule, 52–54